Mindset of Success

How Highly Successful People Think about Goal Setting

Learning from Famous Quotes to Plan Your Life like a Millionaire

Patrick Rahn

For information: www.PatrickRahn.com

ISBN: 978-1523301225

First Edition: Sep. 2015

10 9 8 7 6 5 4 3 2 1

What Others Are Saying...

„Good read. I found it very interesting. Being a life coach, I like to read as many self help books as I can. Patrick has struck the right balance of telling, showing and action! As we know we need to be motivated - therefore Patrick has quotes from some interesting people. He then explains them, and then also gives us action steps to complete.“

- Richard Butler Author and Life Coach

„I am in love with this book! What a motivation. Most importantly, the book shows how mindset can actually predict how people take on challenges , learn, and deal with setbacks, The book shows how mindset affects many domains of life, including setting goals, reaching goals. One thing I think I would benefit from would be some additional exercises incorporating the growth mindset into my own life..! Great book..taught me a lot about people in general but has really helped me“

- Sam, Amazon Customer Review

'I Love This Book! It felt like the author was talking directly to me. All my fears and anxiety were gone after reading this book. The positivity and encouragement was so motivating. The exercises were very useful and I'm looking forward to using them daily to attain my dreams of becoming a song writer“

-Megan Edwards, Amazon Customer Review

CONTENTS

INTRODUCTION 1

*"Setting goals is the first step
in turning the invisible into the visible"*

Tony Robbins

W hen it comes to achieving success, you don't have to reinvent the wheel.

There are many people who've made their marks on the world through achieving incredible success in their work. You can follow in their footsteps and achieve your own success!

Your journey to success can be as simple as going from point A to point B. Or it can be similar to "the long and winding road." But no matter your path, certain elements most likely need to be present for you to achieve ultimate success.

From the outset, it may at times seem that our lives are grinding to a halt.

We go from knowing what we want to lumbering laboriously through every day. Slowly, our motivations seem to fade and we lose the sense of who we are. It is never easy to live with yourself knowing that you came close to what you wanted to achieve but did not quite get there. It is a common feeling among people, but it never means that we must give up. It means that we must reach deep within, find motivation and hang on to the source of hope we find.

You see, the goals we set in life should be a guiding principle in choosing where we want to go and how we need to get there. In the same breath, we cannot choose when we do not know what we want, which basically takes us all the way back to stage one: goal setting.

Have you ever seen yourself as worthy and deserving? Have you ever taken time to think about yourself, really think about yourself and what you want in this life? We all have our dreams. At the same time, we all experience trials in the pursuit of these dreams. What should you do when the odds are stacked solidly against you? You rise from the ashes, you find a reason to move on, and you go back to the very basics and set some goals because good goals are the foundation of a great existence.

Looking around, you will find so many inspiring stories of people who always believed in their goals and worked towards actualization with the knowledge that fortitude opens the door to providence.

More importantly, these people had a strong belief in the power of goal setting. They knew that if they created a solid foundation, then all other things would be a matter of principle. These are the ideals I believe in, and these are the ideas that I wish to inspire out of you with this book.

It is true that the world is fraught with challenges, disaster, and deceit. However, giving up on our goals is never an option. Rolling over and exposing our soft underbellies is not the way to approach our lives. Indeed, what is a man or woman without the dreams that make them who they are? Living without goals is like groping in the dark, not knowing where to step next.

The big question is; where do you turn for inspiration?

Television? You are probably fed up with the commercials.

The internet? Way too many scams.

The thrust of the matter is that all answers are within you. However, to dig such answers out, you need a moment of epiphany, you need a moment to step back and look at yourself within a deeply personal context.

Where are your goals pointed towards?
What do you need to actualize your dreams?
How do you set the goals that are going to make or make you?

These are pertinent questions, and they need careful mulling over.

So I set out hoping that in my own small way, I can trigger that spark, that moment of epiphany.

Before you read on, you have to complete this little exercise: Create a list of all your accomplishments to date

(Do not read on until you've got at least 9 accomplishments)

1._____

2._____

3._____

4._____

5._____

6._____

7._____

8._____

9._____

Take a moment, to have a look at these accomplishments.

Lean back, close your eyes and feel how it felt in that moment.

The greatness, happiness and proud feeling you experienced.

Take these feelings to motivate yourself for even more and greater accomplishments in the future!

Tip: *Do this method every morning and it'll give you the motivation and energy you'll need to succeed. It'll make you more resilient and stronger when you're going to face an obstacle on your journey.*

3 Insane (But True) Inspirational Stories

Have you tried really hard to achieve success but failed every time and have now lost heart for it?

There are countless stories, of people who have made it big in their specific field of work, all of whom have faced many difficulties and failures in their initial years, but a focused mind and a motivation for success has helped them become what they are today!

Take the example of **Michael Jordan**, the most popular basketball player the game has ever seen. He was taken out of his university basketball team in his sophomore year, but that did not affect his will to succeed. He grew even more focused and motivated to achieve his goal and worked hard as per his action plan to become the legendary star he is today!

Lance Armstrong is another great example a professional biker who didn't back down or accept defeat, even when everyone thought that his career was at an end for sure! Diagnosed with testicular cancer and tumors in his lungs and stomach at the young age of 25, this strong professional didn't resign himself to accept defeat in life, rather he kept himself motivated, sought treatment for his condition and made a successful comeback in the field of professional biking.

And who can possibly forget the rags to riches life story of the popular writer **J.K. Rowling**, who acquired acclaim and success through the sheer act of perseverance and commitment. She had a goal in life and she strived to achieve it in the face of all obstacles.

If you have lost all hope, then don't! Your dream life is just round the corner and it is all yours for the taking!

As **Brian Tracy** has effectively summed it up for you,

"Goals are the fuel in the furnace of achievement."

So, if you want success; then set out goals for yourself, schedule a plan of action accordingly and proceed on the path to achievement, taking heart from stories of all the others before you, who tried hard and succeeded in life.

Something Steve Jobs taught me about faith

"Again, you can't connect the dots forward; you can only connect them looking backwards. So you have to trust that the dots will somehow connect in your future. You have to trust in something – your gut, destiny, life, karma, whatever. This approach has never let me down, and it has made all the difference in my life"

Steve Jobs

The idea behind Jobs' quote is significant because he talks about how you can't know everything when you first set out to do something. Jobs believed one just has to have faith that in the scheme of life, what he does will eventually have an impact. Jobs stressed that you must have trust in what you're doing.

When you have that faith, you'll continue your journey, doing what you have faith in. It's only later, down the road, when you can look back and see the impact of your work.

Even though you may not have a complete sense of how what you want to do will fit into the big scheme of things, if you truly feel it's what you should be doing or that it's the right thing to do, then just follow through with your pursuits. Have faith that you're supposed to be doing what you've chosen.

Regardless of whether you believe in destiny or prefer to listen to your gut: what does your internal "trust-meter" tell you to do?

If you trust your instincts that something you want to do will be effective or useful to someone, then pursue it and keep doing it. If you continue in the pursuits you have faith in, you won't be disappointed. Your work will eventually come to fruition.

THE FIRST STEP 2

Finding Your Goal in Life

D o you have a goal in life?

After going through the life stories of famous celebrities, who struggled in their initial years, and emerged victorious in the battle of life, you must certainly have some understanding of the importance of setting goals in life. Right?

Remember, living a life with no purpose makes it a life with no meaning, and you certainly don't want that. What you want is success in life.

You want to be successful and perform to the best of your abilities, and leave your mark in this world. So what are you waiting for? Success is just around the corner, all it needs is dedication, belief in yourself, and most important of all finding and working towards your goal in life.

So dream, and dream big! Set goals in life and work hard to ensure success in life.

You will surely ask, what is the first step towards success? Well, the answer is to discover your passion in life! You will only be able to successfully achieve a goal when it is close to your heart. With no motivation to achieve a goal, you have no chance of being successful.

You need to put your heart and soul into achieving your goal, and if you can't, then that means that you haven't set your goals right. Your goal should be aligned to your purpose in life. It should inspire you, excite you, and prompt you to take action, take your life into your hands, and charge down the road to success with confidence. If your goal doesn't motivate you, then it means it wasn't focused enough.

Never Doubt Your Potential

"Think little goals and expect little achievements.
Think big goals and win big success."
David J. Schwartz

This must be your attitude in life. How will you find your purpose and goal in life, if you continue to doubt yourself, your abilities, and your talents all the time?

Your doubt in your capabilities will lead you to set simple goals which have no connection with your purpose or ambition in life. You will take the easy way out, which will eventually prove to be a major problem, as your heart and mind will not support you to work towards a life goal which is of no interest to you.

So take the plunge. Take a leap of faith. Believe in yourself and set your life's goals, relevant to what you want to achieve.

What Mom Never Told You About Finding Your Passion

What interests you? What are your natural talents? Any specific field or subject which motivates you and inspires every fiber of your body? Is there anything that prompts you to action? Have you carved out a set career path for yourself, and are you driving yourself to reach that far off goal and success?

"Don't aim for success if you want it; just do what you love and believe in, and it will come naturally"

David Frost

He encapsulated one of the most important concepts of being successful, find something you're truly passionate about and do it. If you feel strongly about something, no matter what it is, you'll most likely enjoy perfecting your skills in that field and becoming an authority on your subject matter - fueling your success.

Your chances of being successful greatly increase when you're passionate about what you're doing.

Now you might ask, but how do I find my passion?

Just answer the following questions:

1. **What drives you? What is the driving or ruling element in your life?** *Do you love cars or have a passion for painting? Adopt it as your profession.*

2. **What are you passionate about?** *Does thinking about becoming a pilot sets wings to your soul or the idea of learning to be a world renowned pianist your dream in life? Then find out ways to start off a career in the field of your choice*

3. **What is it that consumes your heart and mind all the time?** *Is it progressing slowly yet surely down a set career path you have in mind, or does it involve the operations of your business?*

4. **What gives your life meaning and without what will you feel stranded and confused in life?** *Do you think that music or painting is your life? Then what are you waiting for? Become the best you can be*

Have you answered these questions?

What did you come up with?

Have you just realized that composing music or completing a book manuscript is the thing that is foremost in your mind? Did you just come to terms with the fact that getting a promotion as a Senior Manager in the company means a lot to you? Do you now know that your main goal in life is to propel your business to new heights of success?

If yes, then you have successfully passed the first obstacle. Once you discover your passion, all you have to do is just keep doing it to achieve success.

For example:

- If you loved to work on cars as a teen, figure out a way to continue your mechanical pursuits and get paid for them as an adult.

- If you're passionate about baking cookies and cakes, bake plenty of these pastries and sell them.

You see, when you do what you love, you'll enjoy the time you spend doing it. Plus, you'll be compelled to experiment more with your chosen work and become better and better at whatever it is you're doing. Your confidence will surge and so, too, will your success.

Try these tips to bring more of what you love into your work life:

- What do you enjoy most? If your current career isn't one of your choices, then consider bringing one of your hobbies into your work life. By building a career around a beloved hobby, you'll enjoy your work considerably; then work will be more like play. Rather than quitting your job to do your hobby, try building a side income with your hobby first.

- How can you monetize it? Determine several ways you can make a profit from your hobby. Could you sell what you make? Could you teach others your skills? Could you start a related business selling hobby supplies to others? Could you start a website where you discuss your hobby and sell advertising on it to bring in regular income?

Get started. Whatever plans you make for turning what you love into your work, take action towards making it a reality. For example, if you want further education or certification in your chosen line of work, enroll in a class. If you're going to sell what you make, make some items and sell them - you could use Craigslist, eBay, put up a website, and more

Understanding Reasons behind Your Passion

So have you decided what you're passionate about? Know what it is that you want to achieve? That's good because you are no longer part of the confused population that has no idea what is their purpose in life is.

The next step is for you to understand the relevant reasons behind your Passion. If your ultimate goal in life is to carve out an outstanding career for yourself, and also have small ambitions linked to it, then do you know the reason behind your motivation?

It is important to know the main reasons behind your goals, as it will define your driving force which governs all your decisions. Once you know why you need to achieve a goal, you will be more motivated, ambitious, focused and driven to work hard to achieve an ambition.

Find Your Main Driving Force

Is your main reason and driving force:

- Money?

- The urge to prove yourself and your talent in the world?

- Do you want to be a business tycoon?

- The initiator of a major change?

- Want to contribute to society?

- Is personal satisfaction the driving force behind your goals?

- Do you believe it to be your duty to make the world a safer and better place for future generations?

Whether your reason involves a philanthropist intention or a way to enhance your self esteem, having a clear idea of why you are striving for a definite goal, will help to make you more **focused**, **determined** and **energized** efforts to achieve your goal.

Once you have pinpointed the actual cause and reasons for your ambition, evaluate them.

Are your reasons valid, and true to your heart and everything that you want to do in life? Are they in line with your set goals? Is there any room for improvement, addition or pruning in your goals or the reasons behind your ambitions?

Action Commitment

Write down one specific thing you do differently as from now of what you've learned so far!

(i.e. : from now on every morning I wake up and I'll list at least 5 thinks I am grateful for, BECAUSE this will give me the motivation and energy I need to succeed.)

_____

_____

_____

_____

_____

_____

_____

_____

_____

_____

_____

_____

_____

3

> *"Setting a goal is not the main thing. It is deciding how you will go about achieving it and staying with that plan."*

Tom Landry

Arrange Everything at the Start

Adjust details in this initial stage. Don't wait till you're halfway there and then try to think back, change your reasoning and modify your goals according to it. It will add confusion to your life. You might get stranded halfway unsure of the next step to take towards that desired goal, which was once as bright as the North Star in the sky, but has now become as hazy as a foggy landscape!

Plan in the initial stages! Have a clear idea of what you want to do in life and how you wish to achieve it. With a sound reasoning to govern your steps in life, and to boost your self-confidence and self-esteem, you can soar to success and achieve excellence in life just as your heart desires!

Never settle for anything less than the very best you can do! Always soar for the skies, and for that, you need to have a solid foundation which is possible only when you believe in your goal and your cause more than anyone else!

Be determined and let your reasons be the guiding force in life!

Identifying Resources Needed for Success

"To succeed in your mission, you must have single-minded devotion to your goal."
A.P.J. Abdul Kalam

So, are you ready with a definite and clear goal in mind? Have you decided what you want to do in life? Have you outlined the small goals which will help you reach the main objective, which is your driving force in life?

While finding your purpose in life is undoubtedly the first thing you need to do in order to enjoy success, your efforts don't end there. After crossing one milestone, you need to get ready for the next one in line. And that is to pinpoint the resources you will need to achieve your desired success in life!

Without the right resources, you will have a hard time trying to work towards your goal. Whether you have a new business plan in mind or are working for the achievement of a personal goal, you need the right resources for it.

Once you have the determination and direction, let's work on how you will get there.

To start off a new venture, get admission in a top notch professional college, pass your exams with flying colors, achieve the next milestone in your career, and to opt for any community service, you need the proper resources; resources which will aid you throughout the entire process to help you achieve success at the end. So, what can you do?

Find the best resources to help you in your quest. Think of these resources as your light sabers, your super powers, and amulets, which will help advance you by leaps and bounds towards your goals, leaving all obstacles behind!

Want to know what resources you can use to guarantee your success?

Here are 10 great options

1. Find a Mentor
2. Personal Planner
3. Calendars and To-Do Lists
4. Personal Assistants
5. Sense of Commitment
6. Dedicated Spirit
7. The Urge of Success
8. The Spirit to strive
9. Discipline
10. Hard work

1. Find a Mentor and Copy and Paste His Success

A successful American businessman and fearless investor, Warren Buffett has identified one of the most important tips for being successful: seek mentors.

> *"It's better to hang out with people better than you. Pick out associates whose behaviour is better than yours and you'll drift in that direction"*
> **Warren Buffett**

Buffett's quote emphasizes that a person must reach out to those who know more in order to be successful.

Selecting successful people to fraternize with provides you with wonderful role models, free education, and information about how those people excel. As you spend time with them, you'll tend to copy their behaviors, become more motivated, and achieve your own success.

Known for his common sense approach to investing and managing money, Buffett has applied this same mantra when finding mentors to emulate.

Spending time with people who have more knowledge, business savvy, expertise, and even creativity can rub off on you. When you choose to spend time with people you want to be like, you're provided with a treasure trove of information about how those peers work and achieve their goals.

Hanging out with them presents the wonderful advantage to you of being exposed to information that will help you reach your goals. To be inspired, hang out with the best.

Seek and find at least one mentor in your professional field. Soak up all the information he offers. Listen well. Observe how he approaches work and life.

Then try to apply what you see and learn in your own life.

If you want to be more successful, surround yourself with successful people whom you can learn from and model after. You'll be compelled to be successful, just like them.

2. Personal Planners and File Organizer

To keep a track of the things you need to do on time and within a given deadline. Remember, success is just like a train which doesn't stop on a platform for too long. If you miss it, you might have a hard time finding another one which would take you to your desired destination within the time that you have!

So remember, don't miss the train of success, and keep a track of what work you need to do, what short goals you need to meet and all milestones you need to achieve, by planning everything out in your personal planner or organizer.

Write down about the orders you need to complete till the end of the week, which will probably lead to a bigger order from the same vendor. Or jot down the dates on which you need to submit your class assignments, to earn extra credits. Simply note down the order details of your client, contact details of a supplier and inventory list for your home cooking business, so that your work flows smoothly, and you are able to pass one milestone after another, easily!

3. Updated Calendars and To-Do Lists

Another resource you can utilize is your system calendar, which must be updated with all the deadlines you need to meet within the week and the month.

Have to ship an order in two days? Make a point on your digital calendar. Have to submit two projects within the week? Mark the date so that you don't forget. Organize a to-do list, for the week, a fortnight, and the month. This way, you won't miss out any milestone in your life and smile every time you check something off your list as done, as you move one step closer to success! Want to keep all your work in the palm of your hand all the time? Then why not opt for tech savvy resources? A mobile app which lets you organize and plan your day is the perfect resource, which will help you keep all your efforts on track.

4. Personal Assistants

Help from a friend, a sibling or an assistant can help you organize your workload better. With a team of dedicated people around you, working towards the same goal, you can be sure of success.

"The best teamwork comes from men who are working independently towards one goal in unison."
James Cash Penney

Along with all these tangible resources, there are a couple of intangible ones that you need, to bring you ever closer to your goal of success in life. Want to know what they are? Not all important resources are tangible. Some essentials that you need are,

5. Sense of Commitment

How committed are you towards achieving your goal? Are you ready to give it your best? Willing to strive for what you want? If not, then you lack the basic component you need for success.

"The quality of a person's life is in direct proportion to their commitment to excellence, regardless of their chosen field of endeavor."
Vince Lombardi

"Unlike commitment is made, there are only promises and hopes..

but no plans."

Peter Drucker

So, do you have the commitment and the drive to succeed, or do you lack the most vital ingredient for the recipe of success? Sort it out yourself!

6. Dedicated Spirit

"Pursue one great decisive aim with force and determination."

Carl von Clausewitz

Never think that success is attainable even if you don't give your 100%. Success requires toil, hard work and relentless dedication to your dream and goal in life. Otherwise, you can't hope to cross many milestones or progress anywhere on the path to your true ambition.

Remember, if you want it bad, you need to give your all for it!

"Gold medals aren't really made of gold. They're made of sweat, determination, and a hard to find alloy called guts."

Dan Gable

So, do you have all these ingredients? Do you have the golden ingredient dedication in your life? Don't worry. All you have to do is focus all your efforts on one goal and you will fly to meet success!

7. The Urge to Succeed

"The will to win, the desire to succeed, the urge to reach your full potential.... these are the keys that will unlock the door to personal excellence."

Confucius

Do you have the passion and drive to succeed? Do you see only your goal at the end of the horizon, and other milestones leading up to it? If that is so, then you have the urge to reach out and work hard for your ambition.

Without that thirst and need to drive you, you won't take the risk to think out of the box, and let your creativity take wings. When you want something that bad, you give it all you've got! You aren't prepared to take no or impossible for an answer. You just want it and you are willing to do anything and everything to get it! So, are you prepared to overcome every obstacle in your life? Willing to look every person in the eye and defy their claim that you won't succeed?

That's more like it! If you have the guts and urge, you have the booster fuel needed to propel you to success with no hurdles in your path!

"When you want to succeed as bad as you want to breathe, then you'll be successful."

Eric Thomas

8. The Spirit to Strive

Want to strive for something in life? What is it that gets your blood flowing and the creative juices flowing in your mind? What makes your spirits take wings and drives you to put your 200% every time and all the time?

Is it the thought of qualifying for the university football team, or is it the idea of finally living your culinary dream by becoming a professional chef? Your wish to heal the ailing drives your spirit and helps you strive? Or is it the idea of doing a community service that helps you survive all obstacles and weathers in life? Whatever drives you; makes you strive for your ultimate goal.

"You have to always continue to strive no matter how hard things get, no matter how troubled you feel. No matter how tough things get, no matter how many times you lose, you keep trying to win."

LL Cool J

9. Discipline

Is there discipline in your life? Even if you don't follow the iron ground rules which rule the military life, you still need some form of order, restraint and control, so that you are able to take the right decisions in life and effectively work your way to achieving exemplary success as per your desire.

"Discipline is the bridge between goals and accomplishment."
Jim Rohn

Without discipline, your need to succeed and win, and your desire to meet all your milestones in life, will never be met. Do you want to be the star of the football team? Are you planning to secure a promotion in your next company appraisal? Have you dreamed of becoming a pilot, a professional wildlife photographer, a cardiothoracic surgeon or a fashion designer? Well, then how do you hope to make your dreams come true?

Your dream to become a star player will require you to spend extra hours out there on the field.

Your passion to become a doctor will have you poring over books in libraries or doing your best during your residency period. A little discipline in your life will go a long way to advance you on the path towards your goal.

You don't have to do all work and no play, but neither should you get complacent and just spend time without any thought of the impact that your attitude will have on your career, your goals, and your life. If there is no discipline, no order, no routine to life, then you will face major obstacles which can sometimes make it impossible for you to live your dream. And these obstacles will be the result of your own doing!

"We must all suffer one of two things: the pain of discipline or the pain of regret or disappointment."

Jim Rohn

10. Hard Work

It is the most important and the foundation stone of all effort. No goal has ever been achieved without the relentless efforts and sweat being put into a task. If you want to achieve the best there is and shine like a star amongst others, then you need to do something outstanding to stand out from the crowd.

"A dream doesn't become reality through magic; it takes sweat, determination and hard work."

Colin Powell

Without hours of committed and dedicated hard work, nothing is possible and no goals are achievable. Hard work is the secret ingredient that has the potential to make the impossible, very much possible!

"There are no secrets to success. It is the result of preparation, hard work and learning from failure."

Colin Powell

Do you remember the phrase that success is 80% attitude and 20% aptitude? So if you have the positive attitude and the will to succeed, you will win! Hard work will take you there at the end of the rainbow where your dreams will come true.

"Hard work spotlights the character of people: some turn up their sleeves, some turn up their noses, and some don't turn up at all."

Sam Ewing

In the light of this quote, which one are you? Are you one to strive for what you want? Or will you shy away in the face of challenges in life? That is for you to choose. Putting your heart, mind and soul in the game, is the way to success.

Get yourself ready for fun sailing in turbulent waters! The ride will keep you on your toes, but it is guaranteed that it will be action packed fun, with not a single boring moment. And the final reward and destination will be the cherry on top!

Without these tangible and intangible resources, you will have a really hard time trying to set your goals and achieve them. How can you hope to have a beautiful garden without sowing any seeds, choosing good fertilizer or sweating away toweling the sand and weeding the paths? You need to be determined and have a clear idea of what you want, strive to meet deadlines, commit to achieving a new milestone every time, and in short, become the best possible you can ever be!

Without being your best and performing at your level best, how can you hope to be successful in life? With the right resources in your inventory, let's march ahead to the next step!

List all the resources you have:

_____

_____

_____

_____

_____

_____

_____

_____

_____

_____

_____

_____

_____

_____

Learn From Michael Jordan: How To Become a Problem Solving Genius

So, do you have all the items needed in your super checklist to attain success?

If you want to climb to the highest rung of the ladder of success; then nothing less than perfect should never do for you. You should always aspire for the very best you can get in life, and be the very best version of who you are, with all your strengths and weaknesses. Never be a shadow of what you can actually be! Always put your best foot forward and play your perfect game in life. Do you want to go down the pathway to assured success?

Do you have a goal? Do you know what you want? Have you equipped yourself with all the resources you will need to gallop down the road to sure and undeniable success? Do you have such a sharp and clear focus?

"Success is a sum of all steps, repeated day in and day out."
Robert Collier

So are you ready to take all those small steps which will translate into a journey of a thousand steps? Have you developed the needed clarity in mind, required to pursue a clear and unobstructed path to your destined success? If you have; then there is no looking back! You have the solution to getting your desired in life!

All you need to do is step forward with a spring in your step, confident sparkle in your eye and a high self-esteem, and be ready to propel your success into the future! Ready to take the giant leap into the big unknown world? Want to succeed, no matter what the odds may be?

"Just know, when you truly want success, you'll never give up on it. No matter how bad the situation may get."

Unknown

How badly do you want it? Are you willing to put all your effort and resources to achieve your ambition? Has it become the one supreme goal in your life? Does it govern all your actions? Do you want it that bad?

"One of the most important keys to success is having the discipline to do what you know you should do, even when you don't feel like doing it."

Unknown

Now you know what your ultimate solution to real success is.

It is a relentless effort! It is hard work! It is a commitment to your goal. It is painstaking effort whenever it becomes difficult to overcome an obstacle and you still keep on putting your 200% in!

Now you might ask, how do I overcome those obstacles?

Just listen to what Michael Jordan said about confronting and resolving obstacles:

"If you're trying to achieve, there will be roadblocks. I've had them; everybody has had them. But obstacles don't have to stop you. If yo run into a wall, don't turn around and give up. Figure out ho to climb it, go through it, or work around it."

Jordan reminds us that when we're working toward accomplishing goals, we'll run into obstacles. It's necessary to expect them on your road to success. However, you must not be deterred by these obstacles. Instead, confront your challenges, figure out how to resolve the issues, and then fix them.

From the choice of wording, it's clear that Jordan believes if a person is creative enough, he can rise above any obstacle that appears before him. Basically, **Jordan tells us to expect troublesome situations and "figure out" solutions to those roadblocks in order to be successful.**

It's always wise to be prepared. Recognize that it's normal to experience bumps in the road on your way to a better life. Expect these bumps so you won't be shocked or thrown too far from the path when they occur.

You must be willing to confront roadblocks and then tackle them with a vengeance:

- Put on your thinking cap and brainstorm ways to get past your challenge
- Talk to your friends
- Seek advice from your mentor
- Try anything and everything to solve your dilemma

Don't give up or stop until you've figured it out.

Sometimes the most wonderful thing happens when you think your way through an issue: success!

Never looking back! Never thinking of going back the way you have just come! It is all about being clear and focused. Knowing what you want to do. And just doing it!

You want a solution to success in life? Want an easy success formula, a golden recipe, a magic spell to make it all alright and help you carve out a successful career, and happy life in the blink of an eye? Well, get up and smell the potion then! You need to sweat hard, be positive, have a determined attitude and be the best you can be if you wish to find the solution and answer to your quest for success.

"Good things come to those who wait… greater things come to those who get off their ass and do anything to make it happen."

Unknown

Though you do need to be patient and adopt a 'can do' attitude no matter what the odds, it is of infinite importance that you don't adopt a laid back attitude and procrastinate in taking the necessary steps needed. As you wait and work hard, know that the thing you want the most will ultimately come to you. You will get what you want or you will exert every last fiber in your body to get it! Because that is how much you want it, right? That is how committed you are to making your dreams come true, and seeing them translate into a reality! Your solution is in your answer to success!

Well then, full steam ahead, aspiring successor, and the next story of success shall be yours!

List all the obstacles you are facing right now which are holding you back from achieving success!

_____

_____

_____

_____

_____

_____

_____

_____

_____

Now go back to your resource list and choose as many resources you have, to crush an obstacle. The more resources you find for each obstacle, the more likely you'll succeed.

Write it down like this:

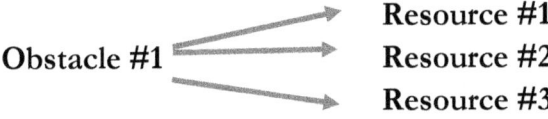

Obstacle #1   **Resource #1**
Resource #2
Resource #3

Action Commitment

Write down one specific thing you do differently as from now of what you've learned so far!

_____

_____

_____

_____

_____

_____

_____

_____

_____

_____

_____

_____

_____

_____

_____

_____

STEP THREE

4

"Most impossible goals can be met simply by breaking them down into bite size chunks, writing them down, believing them, and then going full speed ahead as if they were routine."

Don Lancaster

So we have finally arrived at the most important step of the process; the why and the how of goal setting. How you can ensure success without a doubt when it comes to setting up goals and carving out a path for yourself in life?

The essentials of goal setting have already been discussed earlier in this book. We have also discussed the important essentials of goal setting you need to watch out for, the basic elements that make a goal, the formula for success, and how you need to fill in your inventory with all the resources that you will need for effective success and goal setting.

Now you need to know,

- Why you need to set a goal,
- How to do it,
- And how to use your goal to succeed

This book has already given some basic and brief answers to all these questions earlier on, but now, we will adopt a stepwise approach.

Why to Set a Goal

Let us approach the first question on the path to success. The WHY question! Why is it that you need to have a goal in mind when you set out on your journey to success? Why is it that you don't need any other provision as importantly as a set goal, in order to achieve your destiny? What makes goal setting the essential ingredient?

Why is it that you can't ensure success without it, but can still ensure victory in life even if you don't have money, prosperity or any other resources?

This is because, you need; a spirit to succeed, the eye to focus on a distant vision and a will to achieve it; more than anything else in the world, if you want to attain success!

You might have all the wealth in the world, and have all the essentials seemingly essential to success, and yet might still find success slipping through your fingers, because you lack the one important thing in life - and that is a set goal!

You need to set a goal in life because you:

- Can give direction to your life, actions and way of thinking

- Know what you want out of life which is the first sure step and milestone to foster critical thinking
- Need a direction and path in life. Don't want to wander around without any ambition for the remainder of your life, do you?
- Want to be a great success in your line of interest
- Want to know the best that you can become and achieve the best you can aspire to be
- Know your own limits, strengths, and weaknesses
- Can learn more about yourself, and become a better you
- Can discover your potential
- Can challenge yourself
- Can give others a run for their potential and money by showing them what you've got and what makes you special

Are these reasons enough for you to try your hand at setting and write down your goals?

Goal Setting Groundwork

"Most impossible goals can be met simply by breaking them down into bite size chunks, writing them down, believing them, and then going full speed ahead as if they were routine."

Don Lancaster

Being all ready to enjoy the fruits of setting meaningful goals in life, it has become more important than ever before for you to understand the groundwork that needs to be done, for your goals to be effective guiding steps towards your ultimate destiny!

"This one step – choosing a goal and sticking to it – changes everything."

Scott Reed

So are you ready to change everything in your life, and live a life that you have always wanted? Do something that you have always wanted to do? Do something that inspires you and is your ultimate passion? Here is how you do it, by laying out the foundation of your goal.

Do the base work well, and you can be sure of building a durable and reliable goal setting groundwork for yourself, and a stable future.

Here's how you do it,

Find Out the Fundamental Key to Success

What is it? The critical key to your success? If you have followed the train of thought throughout this book, the answer should be on the tip of your tongue! It is your passion.

If you miss out on this critical element, then you know that it is all downhill from there. How can you hope to build the solid foundation of a happy future on crumbling goals which keep changing all the time?

You need a solid foundation, something which is only available when you set goals which are in line with your passion in life and are achievable, specific and time bound in nature. Remember, you have to be the very best possible that you are and can really be!

"I am here for a purpose and that purpose is to grow into a mountain, not to shrink into a grain of sand. Henceforth will I apply all my efforts to become the highest mountain of all and I will strain my potential until it cries for mercy."

Og Mandino

Be Focused and Clear About What You Want and How You Will Get It

Without a clear and razor sharp idea of what you want from life and how you aim to achieve it, you won't be able to get anywhere.

"Your goal should be just out of reach, but not out of sight."
Denis Waitley and Remi Witt

With a clear idea of what you want out of life, you will be more committed and motivated to work hard to achieve that goal. Remember, without focus, your battle is lost even before it has even begun!

Assume Responsibility for Your Actions

Always be ready to take responsibility for your actions. This will prompt you to take only calculated and wise decisions, ones that will have a resounding long term impact on your life. With your life and success at stake, you will be motivated to assume responsibility and take prudent yet daring actions.

"A sign of wisdom and maturity is when you come to terms with the realization that your decisions cause your rewards and consequences. You are responsible for your life, and your ultimate success depends on the choices you make."
Denis Waitley

Oprah said, *"I don't think of myself as a poor deprived ghetto girl who made good. I think of myself as somebody who from an early age knew I was responsible for myself, and I had to make good."*

In this quote, Oprah stresses that she never thought of herself as someone who was "poor" or "deprived." She chose not to see herself as disadvantaged in any way.

Instead, she regarded herself as equal to everyone else and, like anyone else, knew she was the one responsible for her own life. Even as a young person, she was compelled to do something with her life. She knew no one else would do it for her.

Oprah brings home the importance of taking control of your own life as early in life as possible. She viewed her personal sense of responsibility as the key to "making good."

Regardless of your background, you can be successful if you take responsibility for your own future.

Consider these ideas:

- Circumstances don't control your future. Refuse to allow your personal situation to color your sense of who you truly are or what you can accomplish.
- Instead, view yourself as capable of achieving anything you set out to accomplish.
- Seek solutions to your challenges so you can keep moving forward toward your goals.

- Your success doesn't depend on luck, where you live, or whether you're rich or poor. It does depend, however, on how you step up to take responsibility for yourself. Avoid blaming others, making excuses, or just wishing things will get better.

Develop Qualities of Successful People in Yourself

So, do you want to be part of the group of successful people? Then work to adapt certain habits which are seen as prerequisite essentials of successful people.

These people have,

- A sound vision
- Are fully aware of who they are
- Know what they want to believe in
- And are well aware of the values and objectives they stand for

With such sound knowledge about yourself, success is sure to follow.

Clarify Your Inner Values

Know yourself and cultivate the values which will help pave the way towards the path of true success. Understand your true worth and potential. Trust your intuitions; examine your present and past behaviors, identify your self-esteem and be ready to live in the truth of who you are and what you aim to become. What are the three most important values, qualities, factors in your life today?

1.)_____

2.)_____

3.)_____

QUICK TIP: If you're not sure about your values:

1. **Make a list of all your friends you hanging around very often with and you trust**

2. **Send each of them a short email asking them what they think your values are**

3. **Compile the results. Write down all the unique core values, overlaps, and trends, and "surprises."**

4. Now write down your "final" core values. Give this

sometime... and don't be afraid to revise and refine them.

With this method, you'll see if your self-image and your actions behave the same way.

Decide What You Want To Do the Rest of Your Life

At this point of carving out a bright future for yourself and setting out a goal in the process, you should know what it is that you want from your life. What it is that you want to do for the remainder of your life?

Are you ready to live as an expert technical guide or does a career as an evolutionary author, excite you? Know what it is that will fuel your passion and existence all your life. Find out now! There is never a better time.

Strive To Become an Expert

Whatever field you choose, strive for excellence in it. Associate with the experts to improve your understanding and exposure of the field. This way, you will be able to set better and more realistic goals, and strive to achieve them.

"Peak performance begins with your taking complete responsibility for your life and everything that happens to you."

Brian Tracy

These 7 Goal Setting Questions Can Change Your Life

Are we all set and clear on the importance of a goal in your life?

Want to know how to channel the inner strength and potential in your life? Want to know how to achieve all that you can? Well then, all you have to do is to set a goal and set it right, and your life will then have a direction, a purpose and a drive, all in one!

The biggest question that you are undoubtedly facing at the moment is how to set your goal in life. Yes; you have recognized the ultimate importance of such a direction to your life. Yes; you know what you need to succeed in life, but the one question is; how do you actually do it?

Just make sure you write your goals down only written goals are really goals otherwise it's just a dream. You must write them in presentness like you already achieved them and they must be SMART:

Specific – Your goal should have a defined and set ambition. Know what you want in life. There is strictly no room for vagueness and confusion.

For example, if you want to be successful, then don't have a goal like 'I want to be a famous basketball player", instead go for 'I want to be a famous NBA player.'

Measurable – Your goal should give you a guideline of how you will achieve success. What deadlines or targets do you need to meet and how do you need to improve your skills set?

You will have a goal like 'I will become an NBA player by practicing with the best coach and qualifying for the university team by the end of the year.'

Achievable – Just be realistic and don't go haywire with your goals. While you need to dream big, just don't dream about goals that will utilize all your efforts and leave you frustrated with no rewards. Take all the factors into consideration and make an informed choice.

Focus on 'I will be a really good player and learn from my peers. I will utilize my talents to become a valuable asset to the team.' Don't be like, 'I will beat all my peers and become the best player in the world.'

Realistic – Have a goal towards which, you will be willing to work and have the ability to perform.

An example is, 'My passion for the game will guide me and be my driving force. My natural talent with hard work will help me to achieve success.' Rather than, 'I am the best and will attain worldwide fame in my very first game.'

Timely – Your life's goal should have a timeframe, giving you a timeline of how you aim to achieve success with small achievements throughout your life, which will ultimately lead to the achievement of your dream in the long run.

'I will qualify for the varsity team in the initial semesters of my time there, and will become a star player within 2 years.' Rather than, 'I will qualify for the varsity team soon and be on the road to success after that.

To achieve greatly in life, you need to be clear about your goals in all areas of your life:

Personal, Family, Business & Career, Financial and Health

It is important you answer all the question below.

When you set your goals, imagine you have no limitations.

List your three most intensely desired personal goals:

1.)_____

2.)_____

3.)_____

List your three most intensely desired Family goals:

1.)_____

2.)_____

3.)_____

List your three most intensely desired Business & Career goals:

1.)_____

2.)_____

3.)_____

List your three most intensely desired Financial goals:

1.)_____

2.)_____

3.)_____

List your three most intensely desired Health goals:

1.)_____

2.)_____

3.)_____

Imagine you could be absolutely guaranteed of success in any of your goals in the next year, which one goal would you choose?

_____

Write out your goal in detail — make it clear, specific and measurable:

_____

_____

_____

_____

Use the flowchart below to ensure that your Goal is "SMART" enough and capable of being achieved.

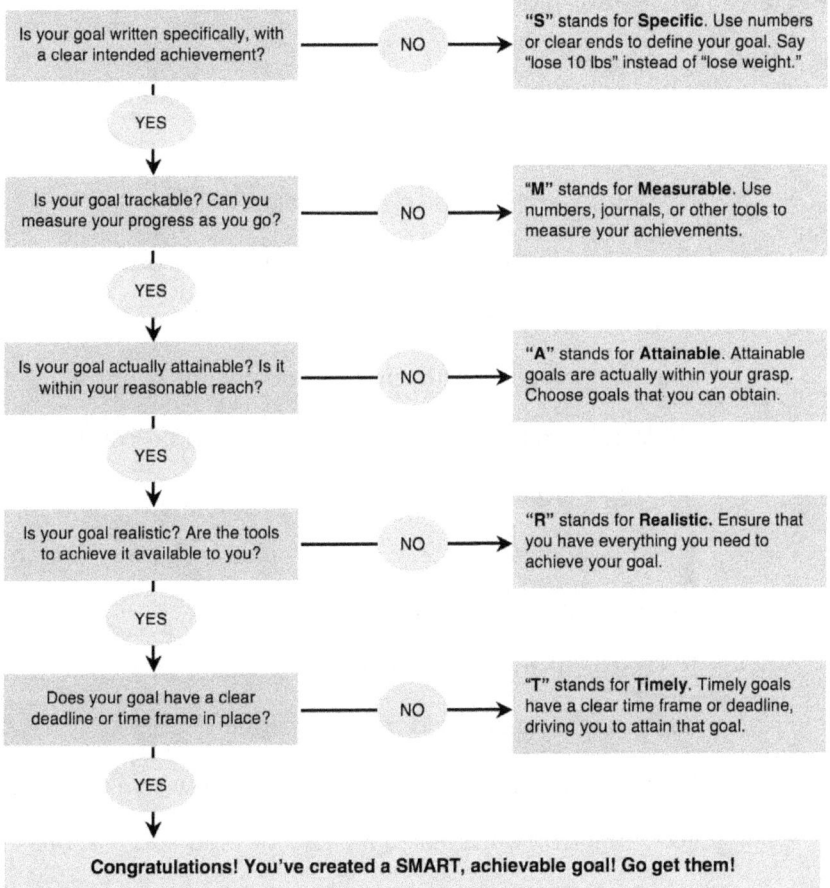

Is your goal written specifically, with a clear intended achievement? — NO → "S" stands for **Specific**. Use numbers or clear ends to define your goal. Say "lose 10 lbs" instead of "lose weight."

YES ↓

Is your goal trackable? Can you measure your progress as you go? — NO → "M" stands for **Measurable**. Use numbers, journals, or other tools to measure your achievements.

YES ↓

Is your goal actually attainable? Is it within your reasonable reach? — NO → "A" stands for **Attainable**. Attainable goals are actually within your grasp. Choose goals that you can obtain.

YES ↓

Is your goal realistic? Are the tools to achieve it available to you? — NO → "R" stands for **Realistic.** Ensure that you have everything you need to achieve your goal.

YES ↓

Does your goal have a clear deadline or time frame in place? — NO → "T" stands for **Timely**. Timely goals have a clear time frame or deadline, driving you to attain that goal.

YES ↓

Congratulations! You've created a SMART, achievable goal! Go get them!

"Goals are your destinations in life; objectives are the stops along the way."

Gerard de Marigny

When you set a goal, just check whether it has all the following characteristics or not. If your goal lacks anything, work on it. If it answers the checklist perfectly, then make it the one objective in your life to work upon, to overcome every milestone and achieve success with flying colors!

Here's what your goal needs to have, and how you need to assess it,

- Does your goal inspire you

- Is your goal in line with your passion in life

- Do you feel motivated to work to achieve your goal

- Have you outlined smaller goals which will help you attain the bigger, all important objective of your life

- Do you wish to go the extra mile every time you feel the drive to succeed in life

- Is your goal a specific, time-bound, relevant, passion focused, and achievable endeavor

- Is your goal in life all focused on what you want out of life? Or is it just copied from someone else?

- Have you outlined an action plan for how you will work according to your goal to achieve desired success, or is it just a thought in your mind?

After answering all these questions, you will have a somewhat clearer idea of what kind of goal you need to set for yourself.

If your goal is not passion driven, then it is not your goal in life. It doesn't drive you; therefore, it is of no use to you. You want something else and your goal is directing you towards another path. With such a glaring contrast between what you want and do, it becomes impossible for you to achieve anything in life, let alone succeed!

For success, your thoughts, mind, and efforts need to be focused on one main centre, which is your ultimate goal. With no harmony in thought and mind, you will be pulled in different directions with a magnetic field which will never let you concentrate on what you want and how to achieve it. You will be stuck without a direction and no compass to guide your path.

Don't do that to yourself. Have a goal which is in line with what you want in life. Know what you want, how you wish to achieve it, and how you will work your way, step by step, to go where you need to!

Action Commitment

Write down one specific thing you do differently as from now of what you've learned so far!

_____

_____

_____

_____

_____

_____

_____

_____

_____

_____

_____

_____

_____

"Action springs not from thought, but from a readiness for responsibility."

Dietrich Bonhoeffer

Developing Scheduled Plan of Action

A re you ready to take action? Are you ready to put in effort, so that you can realize all your goals and ambitions in life? To make it all work, you need to have a plan of action at hand at all times. Otherwise, you will be making big plans and achieving nothing at all.

"Intention without action is an insult to those who expect the best from you."

Andy Andrews

To define your plan of action, you need to take certain crucial steps. Without having and acting on a definite plan of action, you can say goodbye to all your little dreams and ambitions, for sure!

Importance of Proper Planning

Can you achieve something as important as your goal in life, without a definite course of action or a plan in mind?

No!

When you plan even the smallest detail of a trip you intend to take; then why not plan out the finer details of your life? Why not think about what you want to do in life, what milestones you will have to achieve, what efforts you will need to make, the level of struggle and hardships you will have to face to get something that you have always wanted?

Plan out your life! It is that important, isn't it? Don't you think it makes sense to take out time and carve out a complete plan, of what you want to achieve and how you will proceed step by step in life?

"Our goals can only be reached through a vehicle of a plan, in which we must fervently believe, and upon which we must vigorously act. There is no other route to success."

Pablo Picasso

How to Plan and Devise an Action Strategy in Life

Don't worry. It's not as difficult as it looks. In order to define a plan, the first thing is that you should have a very clear idea of what you want in life.

Once you have an objective, focus all your attention on it. Now with a goal in mind set out to find possible paths and lines of action, which will ultimately end in the achievement of your desired goals. What steps in succession will bring you closer to your ultimate goal in life?

Use My **Visual Skyrocketing Success** technique to plan out your goals. I created this technique to clearly visualize my plan of goals on a single piece of paper to maximize my success. The big benefit of this method is that it'll hold up your motivation and focus, because you can immediately see what and when you have to do something without going through a whole goal setting manifesto, like before.

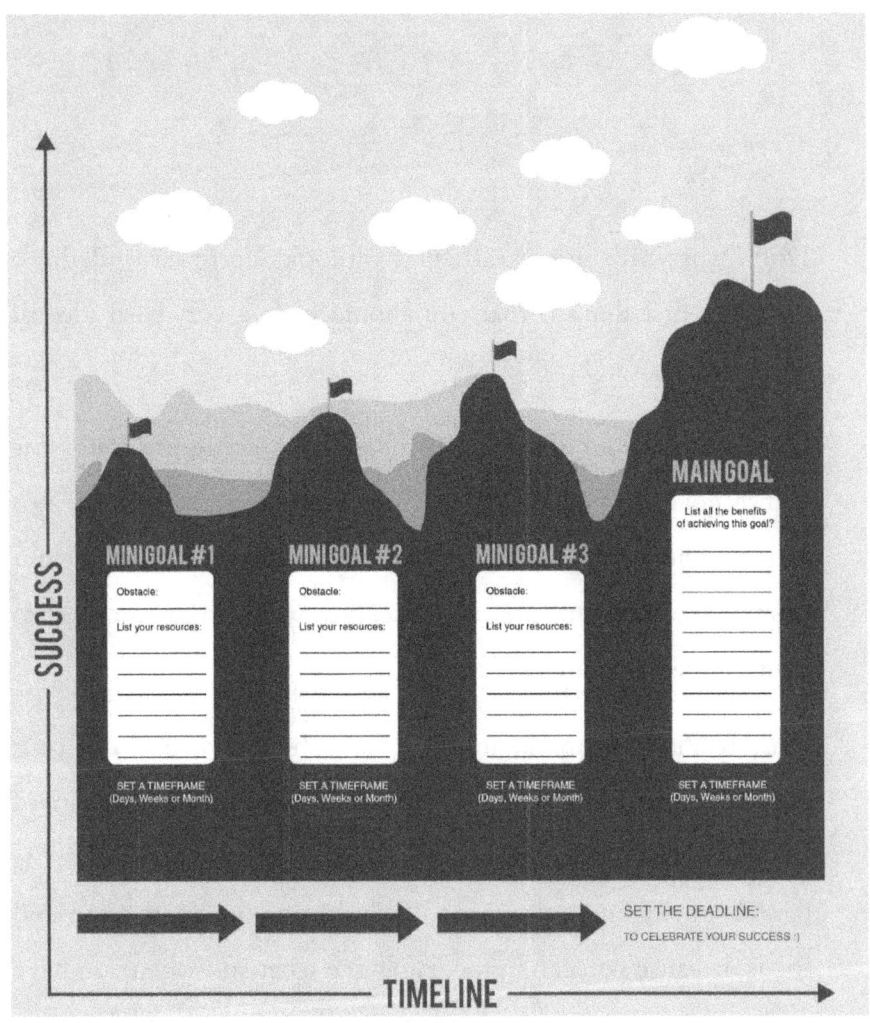

QUICK TIP: When you plan out your Goals with the VSS Technique, put it on your Fridge or nearby your workplace where you can see it every day. It will help you visualize your desired outcome, by staying motivated and focused and this will increase your success rate by 200%.

Will your goal to become a celebrated author become a reality if you join creative writing lessons or will it be a good idea to seek professional career counseling before you decide for sure? That is for you to decide. You are the best judge of how you aim to get to your goal. Only you know how far you are willing to strive for that dream!

To have a plan of action which is both effective and efficient, make sure that your plan is,

- Focused
- Goal centric
- Highly detailed
- Realistic
- And last yet, but not the least – inspiring!

With such an action plan, you will be able to meet goals, and strive for success as desired!

Exercise Self-Control

Do you have the perfect plan of action outlined but yet fail to achieve your desired dream? Why?

Because, there is a stark difference between making a plan and sticking to it! You need an infinite amount of self-control; otherwise you will end up having a perfect plan, with you being no closer to attaining your dream.

Your self control is the key to your long term happiness, power, confidence and overall personal wellbeing. One way to have self control is to keep your focus on the prize.

How to Succeed

Want to know the formula for success? It's easy! Just proceed step by step on the path you have planned out for yourself, and don't falter whenever an obstacle gets in your way!

Just work hard, put in your best effort and proceed with every fiber of your body committed to achieving what you have always wanted in life. Just be yourself, hold true to yourself, your dreams and ambitions.

Set goals which help you get one inch closer to your ultimate goal in life, and just aim for the success you have always wanted!

Always remember,

"Nothing is impossible; the word itself says I'm possible!"
Audrey Hepburn

It's just how you look at it. You can just sit back and think that the obstacle in your path is going to ruin all your dreams and ambitions, or you can work hard to consider it as an opportunity in disguise. It's your call! It's how you aim to see things in life and work to achieve your goals.

Never think that your goal is impossible to achieve because it is you who can, and will, make everything possible. If you want something that bad in life, why take the backseat when it is your life! Why not become your own catalyst for a change? Why not just become the initiator of an era of happiness and prosperity in your life? Why not just be ready to live for once, with nothing holding you back and with every fiber in your body offering you the strength you need to work towards your goal? Why not become the most awesome and great 'you' you can be?

"You are afraid to die, and you're afraid to live. What a way to exist."
Neale Donald Walsh

Don't be! Live to achieve success and your dreams. Nothing should be holding you back! Not even yourself. Your goals should be the beacons of hope that serve as guiding lights on the path of sure success in your life. You should have a never-ending reservoir of energy to guide you to attain your goals.

"Even the greatest was once a beginner. Don't be afraid to take that first step."
Unknown

The most important question to ask yourself is,

"Do you give as much energy to your dreams as you do to your fears?"
Unknown

Always remember, you have everything that all other great people before you had. It is now up to you, to take your potential to the next level! Do you now know how to do that?

"Don't say you don't have enough time. You have exactly the same number of hours per day that were given to Helen Keller, Bill Gates, Michelangelo, Mother Teresa, Leonardo Da Vinci, Thomas Jefferson and Albert Einstein."

Unknown

4 Ways of Thinking Positive Makes Your Life Sweeter than Christmas Morning

"Nothing can stop the man with the right mental attitude from achieving his goal; nothing on earth can help the man with the wrong mental attitude."

Thomas Jefferson

Thomas Jefferson was the third U.S. President, the writer of the Declaration of Independence, and a leader. In this quote, Jefferson focused on the importance of one's mindset to achieving success. Jefferson expressed that as long as a person has a positive "mental attitude," he'll continue to strive toward and achieve his goals.

He believed there's power in one's own mind and that being positive is the best way to release that power and benefit from it.

On the other hand, Jefferson acknowledged that a person who lacks a good mental attitude will be thwarted in his efforts to accomplish goals. No matter how hard he tries, if he's not in a positive frame of mind, success will elude him.

These strategies will help you maintain a positive mindset:

- **Use positive self-talk.** You engage in a running dialog with yourself all day long. Take advantage of this natural tendency and encourage yourself by saying things you like to hear. Praise yourself for your accomplishments and say good things to yourself all day long. Soon, you'll notice a positive change in your everyday thoughts as well.

- **Repeat affirmations**. Reading and repeating affirmations will help you strengthen the qualities you wish to develop and even assist you in adopting new habits and qualities. If negative thoughts are a challenge for you, positive affirmations will help steer you away from them and replace them with positivity.

- **Practice meditation**. Meditating will help you reduce the stress in your life, focus on moving forward toward your goals and bring you serenity - all helpful steps for developing and maintaining a positive mindset.

- **Seek the silver lining**. Even when things don't go as planned, find something good in every situation. After a while, this technique will become a habit as you discover your new positivity.

Thinking positive not only makes life a lot more pleasant, but it also sets up an atmosphere around you that's upbeat and encouraging to others and draws others toward you.

When you think positively, you take the mental approach of, "I can achieve whatever I set my mind to." This attitude sets you up for success!

Positive Thinking And Positive Knowing

Though they seem like one and the same thing, they are very different in reality.

How?

Well, positive thinking is a mindset, or a way to train the mind to perceive the reality, by making positive statements on a continuous basis. It is how you learn to perceive the reality around you. You tell yourself that it is all positive and all the hurdles are, in fact, blessings and opportunities in disguise. Well then, how is positive knowing different from it?

In positive knowing, you just know that you will succeed no matter what the odds! The amount of conviction that comes with positive knowing is monumental compared to the positive thoughts you experience in positive thinking.

While knowing that you will succeed, you progress with a spring in your step, self confidence in your body language and a sparkle of self esteem in your eye.

So your aim should be positive knowing,

How to devise a plan of actions easily?

It's easy. Just don't miss out on these important steps,

- Set your goals systematically

- Discipline your life and write down your goals regularly

- Utilize your creativity and brainpower to exert their power and meet your goals

- Develop helpful habits like, **persistence, courage** and **self-discipline** for ensured success in life

- Cast out fear and procrastination. Overcome these obstacles in the path to success before they overcome you!

- Have courage and the will to move forward no matter what the obstacles and hurdles in your way!

March forward, full speed ahead!

TAKE ACTION

"Action is the foundational key to all success."
Pablo Picasso

Picasso's quote reflects that he knew what it would take to be successful. He believed that the most basic tenet to achieving goals is to take action.

Even when people didn't seem interested in his art, Picasso just kept painting, sculpting and creating, no matter what. He put into practice what he believed: if a person takes action, he'll succeed.

The essence of Picasso's quote is, "do something" to make success happen.

You must do something related to your goals if you want to achieve them. The most basic key to accomplishing something is to simply take action.

- Focus less on the details
- Don't be concerned about doing something wrong
- Just get started
- Continue to do whatever it is you've chosen and the actions you take will lead you to success

The most important quality you need to cultivate, which can ensure you lifelong success, is the assured habit of taking actions according to your goals, ambitions and dreams in life.

The harder and more you will try, the more you will succeed!

Action Commitment

Write down one specific thing you do differently as from now of what you've learned so far!

_____

_____

_____

_____

_____

_____

_____

_____

_____

_____

_____

_____

_____

FINAL STEP 6

> *"Success is a journey based on learnable skills!*
> *Learn something new every day and you'll succeed."*
>
> **Patrick Rahn**

After going through this book, you must now have a good idea of what you want in life, what you want to achieve, and how you aim to distinguish yourself in this game of life.

All ready with a set of goals? Has your mind focused on the prize? Do you know what milestones you will cross and the smaller goals you need to achieve in order to get that coveted dream?

Have a definite action plan and are working according to it? Then all your lessons have been learnt well through this book. If you grasped the spirit of this guide; then you have ascended from a sad and a no, can't do attitude to a happy and a go-getter attitude! And that is the ultimate key to success!

"Success means doing the best we can with what we have. Success is the doing, not the getting; in the trying, not the triumph. Success is a personal standard, reaching for the highest that is in us, becoming all that we can be."

Zig Ziglar

Achieving success is a journey. No matter where you are or what you have, you can start your road to success from there. Taking action to do whatever it is you've chosen and putting forth your greatest efforts will move you further in that journey.

The more you try, the more likely you are to achieve your dream. It's unnecessary to try to live up to someone else's standards. Instead, look inside for your own standards and work to achieve them. Be the best you can be and your journey will bring you success.

Your journey to success begins now!

THE AUTHOR

Patrick Rahn is a Marketing and Business Strategist, best-selling author, CEO of Rahn Consulting and a Certified NLP Practitioner who specializes in the art and science of the high-achieving business owner.

Before he founded Rahn Consulting, he had worked in over ten different industries and ended up as a structural engineer with a Master's degree. Because of his journey, and by seeing so many different businesses and industries, he was able to find a common denominator of success – one that became his philosophy: A strong foundation is everything in business as well as your personal life. This is a philosophy that has enabled him to help his clients find underutilized assets and overlooked opportunities to multiply their profits and expand their freedom. Patrick's goal is to help business owners grow their businesses, thereby increasing their freedom and happiness.

Patrick, in his passionate endeavor to help small-to-midsize businesses reach their full potential, invented a process he calls the "Neuro-Business Strategy Process." In this process, he first incorporates his Infinite Personal Growth Triangle. He analyzes the mindset, paradigms, beliefs systems and goals of the business owner.

He then takes his toolbox of proven business tactics and strategies and builds a strategy that fits the business owner, one where they feel happy and free – a company that grows with the business owner on their terms.

Patrick is a best-selling author of the book, Mindset of Success – How Highly Successful People Think About Goal Setting. He has also written books alongside other significant personalities such as New York Times Best-Selling Author, Brian Tracy and five-time Emmy Award winner, Nick Nanton. Apart from writing, Patrick is also the CEO of Rahn Consulting, from where his clients receive the best of his business coaching consulting services. For example, he advises clients from all industries, including Banks, Financial Sales & Services and Award-Winning Tech Companies in Germany.

You can connect with Patrick at:

• www.PatrickRahn.com • Info@patrickrahn.com •

Now ist's on you!

STOP SETTING GOALS ACHIEVE THEM

PATRICK RAHN

PATRICK RAHN

"SUCCESS IS YOUR OBLIGATION"

Find the perfect solution for your obstacle in business, life and the pursiut of success.

READY, SET, GO!

Brian Tracy and Patrick Rahn

Release Fall 2017

www.PatrickRahn.com

www.ingramcontent.com/pod-product-compliance
Lightning Source LLC
Chambersburg PA
CBHW061443180526
45170CB00004B/1540